Welcome to **Chicago!**

Have you seen the city's **big bean?** Color it!

S0-BAI-159

This sculpture is called *Cloud Gate.*
It was created by the artist Anish Kapoor.

Now **doodle** your own **big bean.**

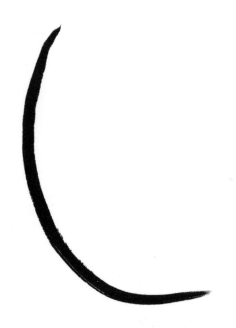

Draw a **thunderstorm** over the city.

The sun has come out. **Doodle a rainbow.**

It's getting **late.** Chicago needs some **stars!**

Doodle some travelers riding on the El.

Doodle a Chicago **El train.**

The Chicago train system is called the El because it is
elevated off the ground.

What's your favorite baseball team?

What would you wear **on your head** to watch
your favorite sport? **Doodle it!**

Turn on the Buckingham Fountain.

Scan this QR code to get coloring pages
made by Graham Fruisen, a kid just like you!

Draw some **butterflies.**

If you like butterflies, visit the Peggy Notebaert
Nature Museum in Lincoln Park.

What is your **favorite show** in Chicago?

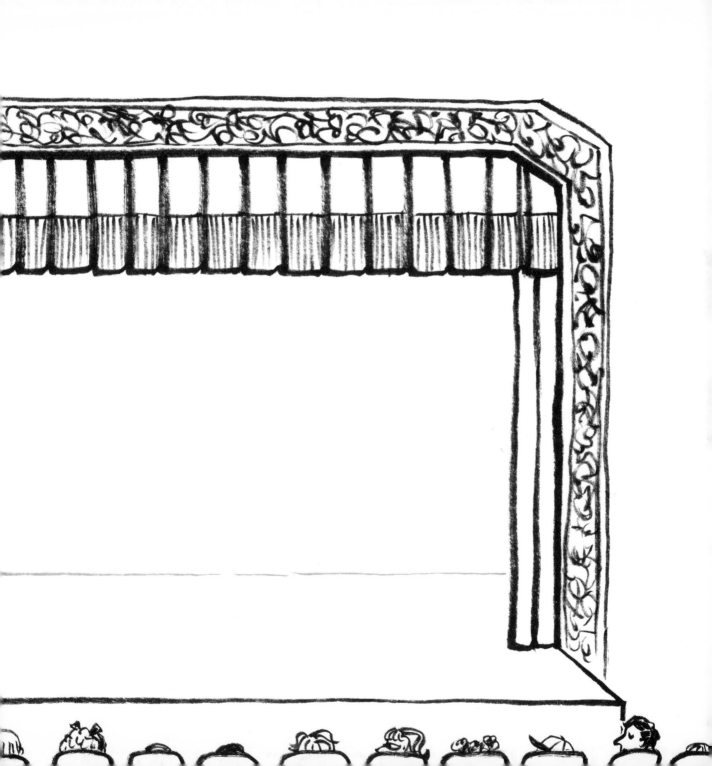

Finish these signs.

Can you name the
honorary street?

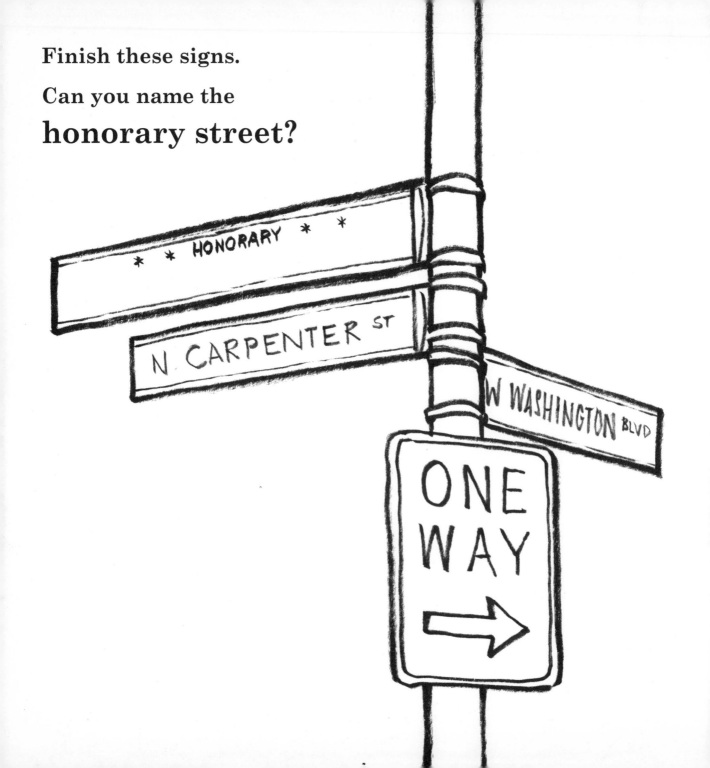

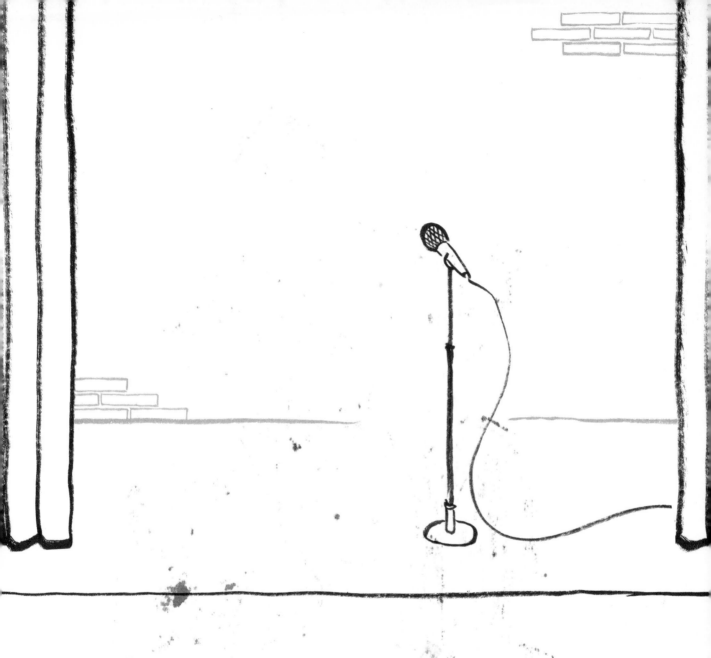

Who is on stage? A comedian? **Doodle it!**

These **people** crossing the street **need faces.**

This **snow globe** needs some **buildings.**

Finish **Sue,** the **dinosaur.**

See Sue, the world's most famous T. rex skeleton, at the Field Museum.

Doodle your own T-shirt.

Scan this QR
code and get more
T-shirts to color!

Who is **performing** at the Chicago Theatre?

It's a **windy** day! **Doodle a design** on this scarf and color it before it blows away.

What **farm animals** are in the barnyard?

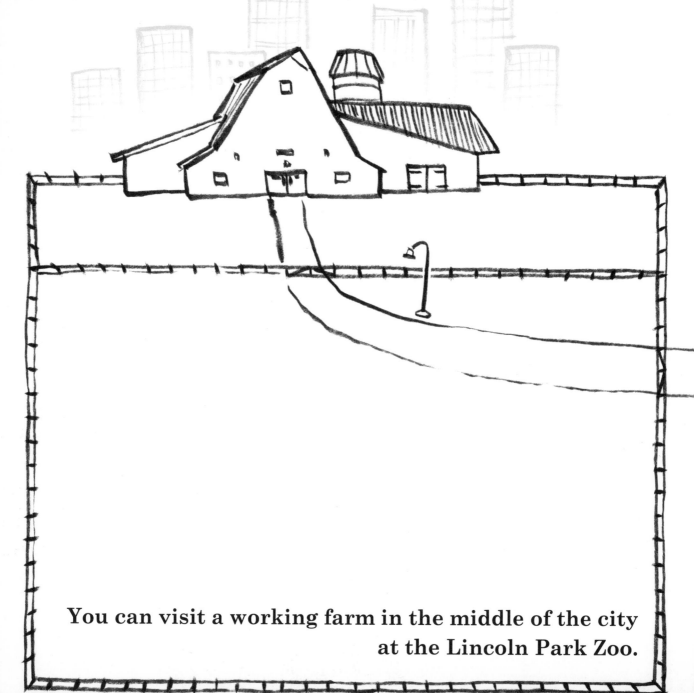

You can visit a working farm in the middle of the city at the Lincoln Park Zoo.

Doodle fish around the coral reef. Color the coral.

Do you like sharks,
jellyfish, beluga whales,
and seahorses?
You will find them
at the Shedd Aquarium.

Finish the snake.

What's going on at the dolphin show?

You can see lots of different animals, from snakes to dolphins, at the Brookfield Zoo.

This boat needs **sails.**

You can see many sailboats from Lake Shore Drive.

The Picasso sculpture looks like a **doodle!**

Can you doodle your own **crazy** sculpture on the platform?

What can you see from the **top** of the **Willis Tower?**

The Willis Tower is really tall. It stands 1,450 feet.

Take the **Doodle Challenge:**

Turn the book upside down, but draw the bean *(Cloud Gate)* **right-side up.**

Look for 4 more Doodle Challenges ahead!

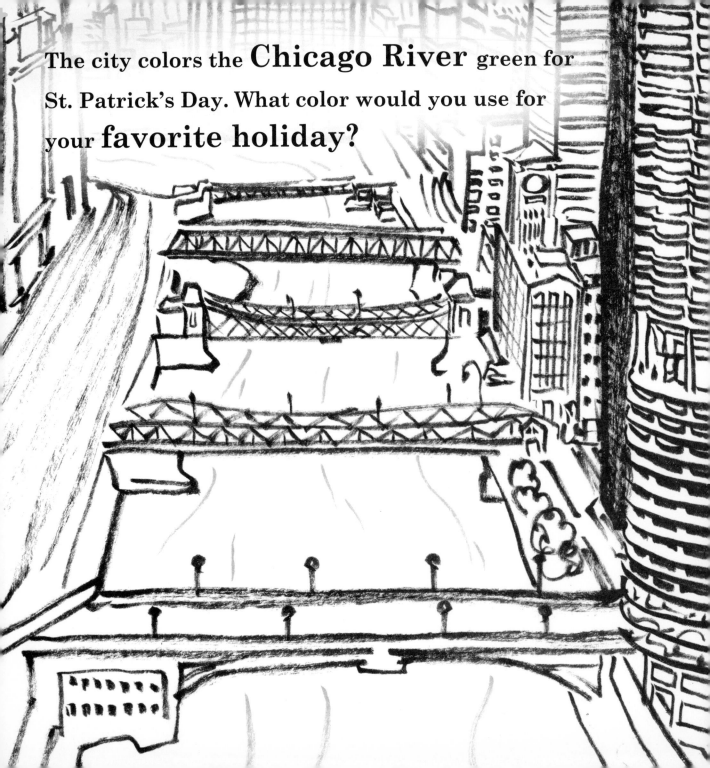

The city colors the **Chicago River** green for St. Patrick's Day. What color would you use for your **favorite holiday?**

Doodle the craziest thing you've seen in Chicago.

Watch out! Somebody's car is getting towed!
Doodle it!

Be careful where you park.
Chicago tow trucks are everywhere!

Doodle passengers on the bus.

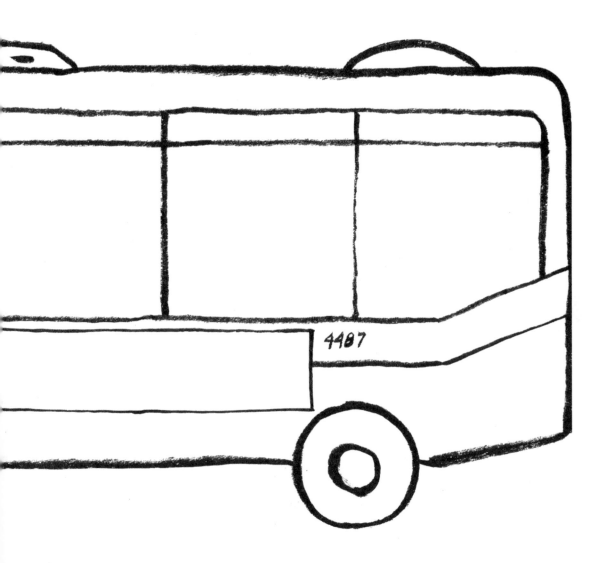

CTA is short for **C**hicago **T**ransit **A**uthority.

Now doodle **your own** bus.

Scan this QR code
and get more cars and
trucks to color!

This **messenger** needs a **bicycle.**

Doodle your own highway map.

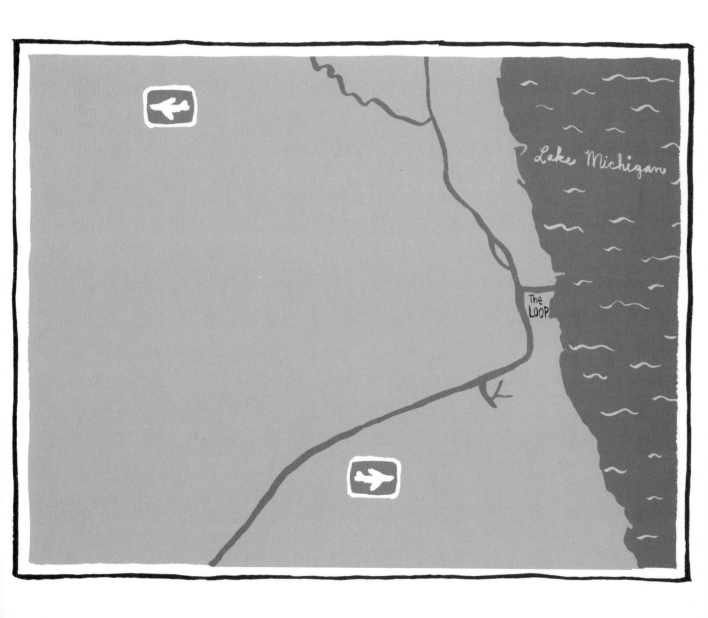

Doodle some planes landing at
O'Hare International Airport.

It's teatime. What will you be having?

Tea is served every afternoon at the Drake Hotel.

Give these **nails**
color and cool designs!

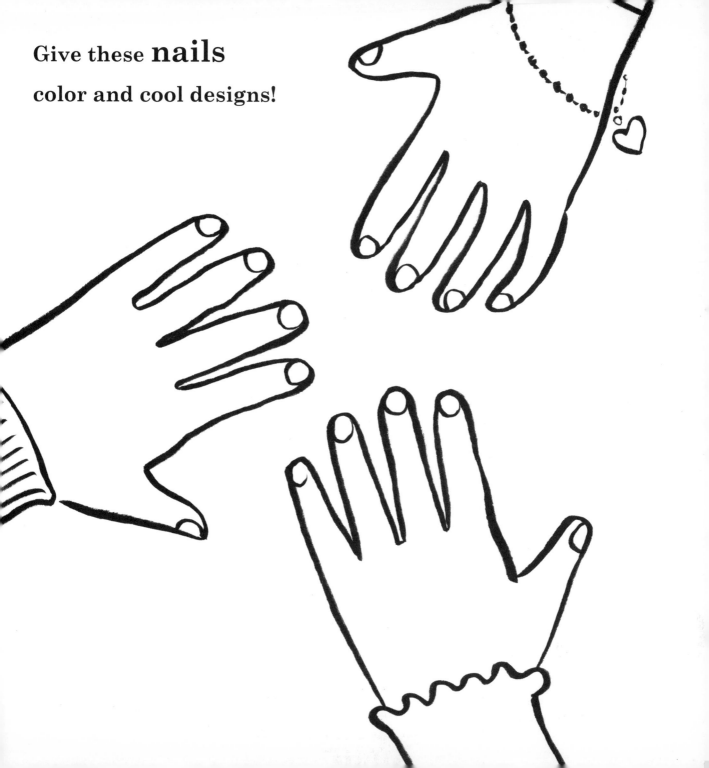

Doodle some shopping bags.

What did you buy on the **Magnificent Mile?**

Shoppers call Michigan Avenue the Magnificent Mile.

Draw the cover of your own book.

My
Chicago Story

Take the Doodle Challenge:

Draw the big bean with your eyes closed.

Look for 3 more Doodle Challenges ahead!

The **bridges are up,** but where are the boats?

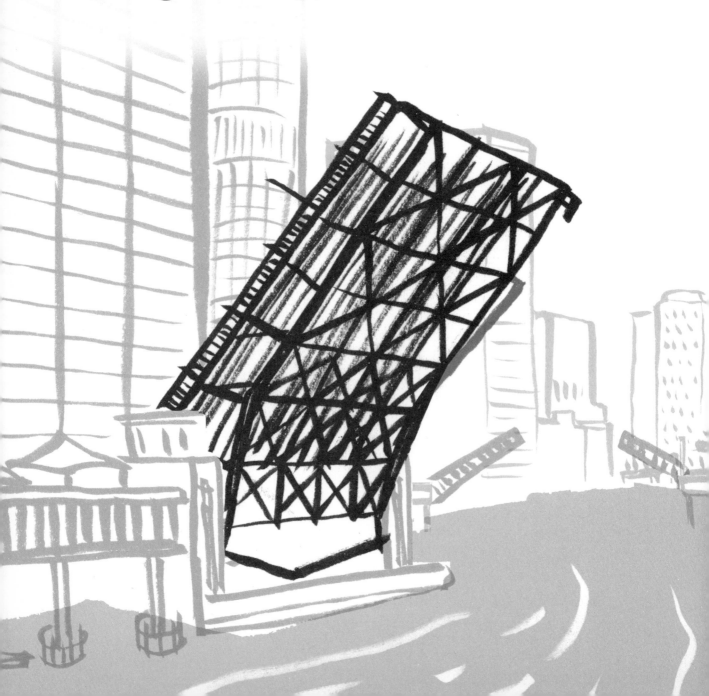

There are many lifting bridges in downtown Chicago.

Doodle the name and number of your
favorite **Chicago Cubs** player.

Doodle the name and number of your favorite
Chicago White Sox player.

A **Chicago-style** hot dog has yellow mustard, green relish, chopped onions, tomato slices, pickled peppers, a dill pickle wedge, and celery salt, all on a poppy seed bun.
Doodle it!

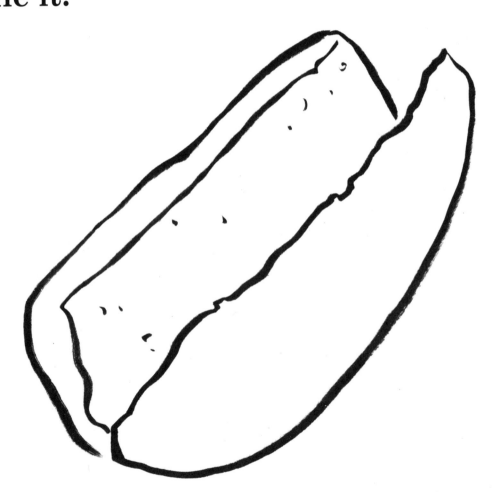

When people in Chicago want all the toppings, they say, "Drag it through the garden!"

Now **doodle** your favorite type of hot dog.

Scan this QR code
and get more foods
to color!

Fill this pan with a deep-dish pizza.

The first deep-dish pizza was baked in 1943 at Pizzeria Uno in Chicago.

This **food truck** needs a name, a menu, and your favorite food!

What is your **favorite** kind of donut?

Take the Doodle Challenge:

Draw the big bean with your left hand if you are right-handed, or draw it with your right hand if you are left-handed.

Look for 2 more Doodle Challenges ahead!

Finish the **Ferris wheel** at Navy Pier.

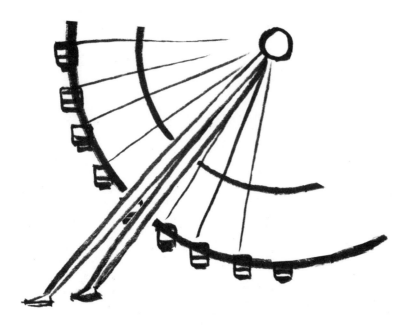

The world's first Ferris wheel was built for Chicago's
1893 Columbian Exposition.

Where are the palm trees in the **Crystal Garden?** Draw them!

Visit the Crystal Garden and the dancing fountains at Navy Pier.

Everybody is **waiting** in line.

Add a statue to the top of the
Board of Trade Building.

The statue on top of this building is Ceres, the Roman goddess of grain.

Would you like to ice-skate in **Millennium Park?**

Make a doodle!

The McCormick Tribune Ice Rink is open from November to March in Millennium Park.

Can you **doodle** like **Frank Gehry?**

This is the Jay Pritzker Pavilion in Millennium Park.
It was designed by architect Frank Gehry.

Doodle some sunbathers.

What is your favorite Chicago beach?

Who is winning the **Chicago Marathon?**

Thousands of runners participate
in the Chicago Marathon each October.

Doodle the name and number of your favorite Chicago Bears player.

Winter is here – time to bundle up.
These four people need hats, coats, earmuffs, and scarves.

American Gothic needs a frame.

This famous painting by Grant Wood hangs at the
Art Institute of Chicago.

Doodle your own *American Gothic.*

The barrel cactus is missing its thorns. Doodle them.

You can see thousands of interesting plants at the Garfield Park Conservatory.

Even the dogs have a beach in Chicago!
Doodle a dog or two.

If your pet likes to swim, visit the Dog Beach at
Montrose Harbor.

Doodle a float for the Bud Billiken Parade.

The Bud Billiken Parade is held each August to signal the end of summer and the beginning of the school year.

Now, make **your own** parade!

It's the 4th of July!
Doodle the Grant Park fireworks over Navy Pier.

Take the **Doodle Challenge:**

Draw your own reflection in the big bean.

Look for 1 more Doodle Challenge ahead!

What do you see in the **Chinatown** window?
Doodle it.

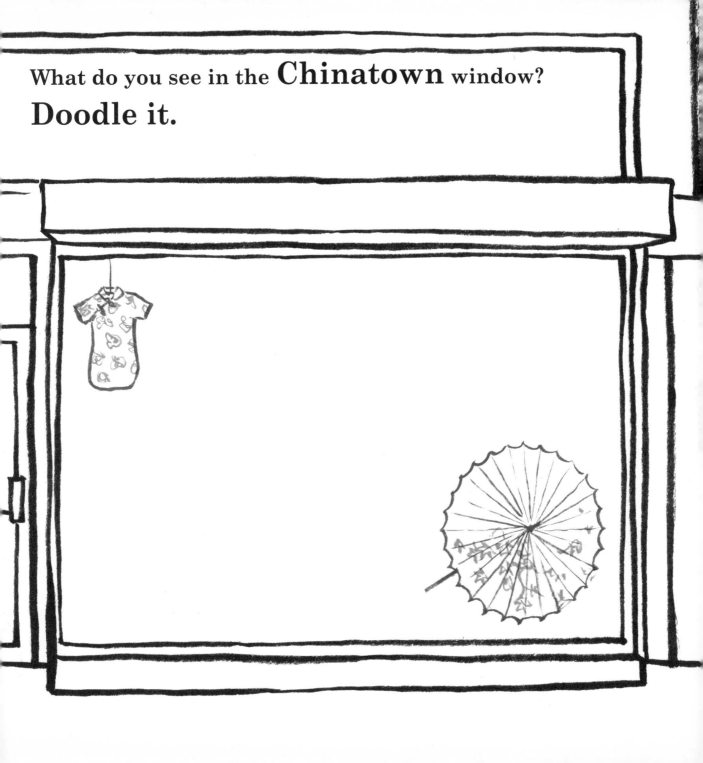

This **stage** needs some **ballet dancers.**

If you like dance, you will love the Joffrey Ballet.

This **concert hall** needs an **orchestra.**

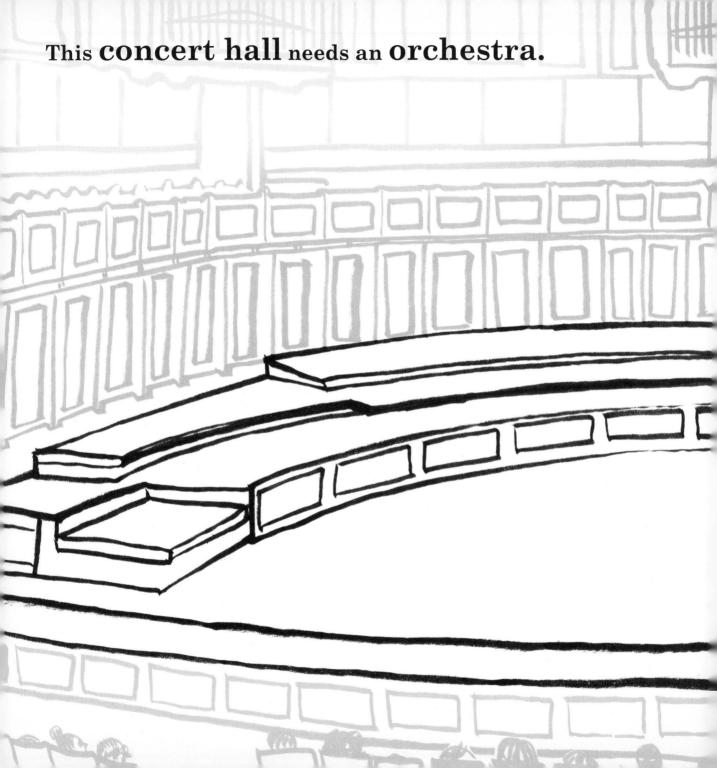

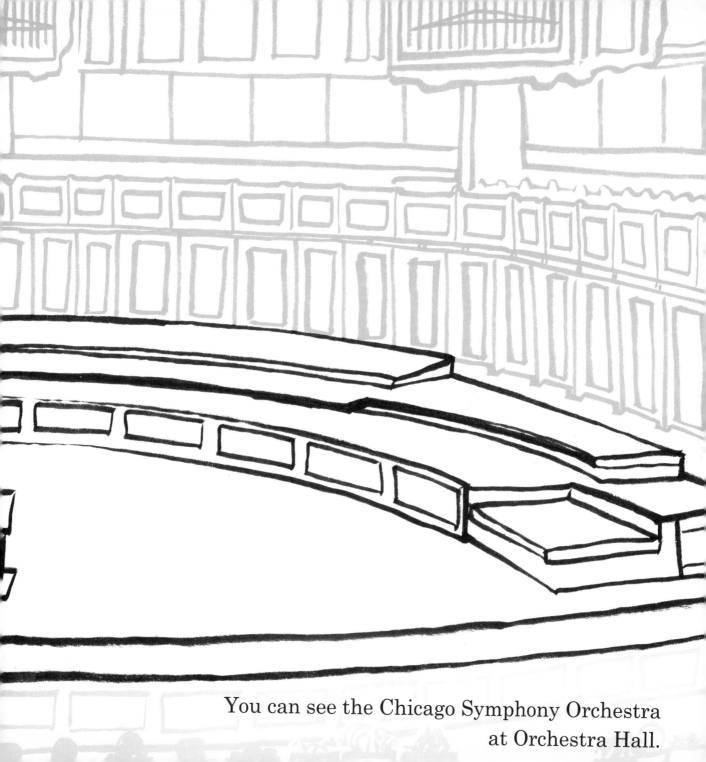

You can see the Chicago Symphony Orchestra
at Orchestra Hall.

What would you do at a block party? Doodle it!

Can you **doodle** the lion in front of the **Art Institute of Chicago?**

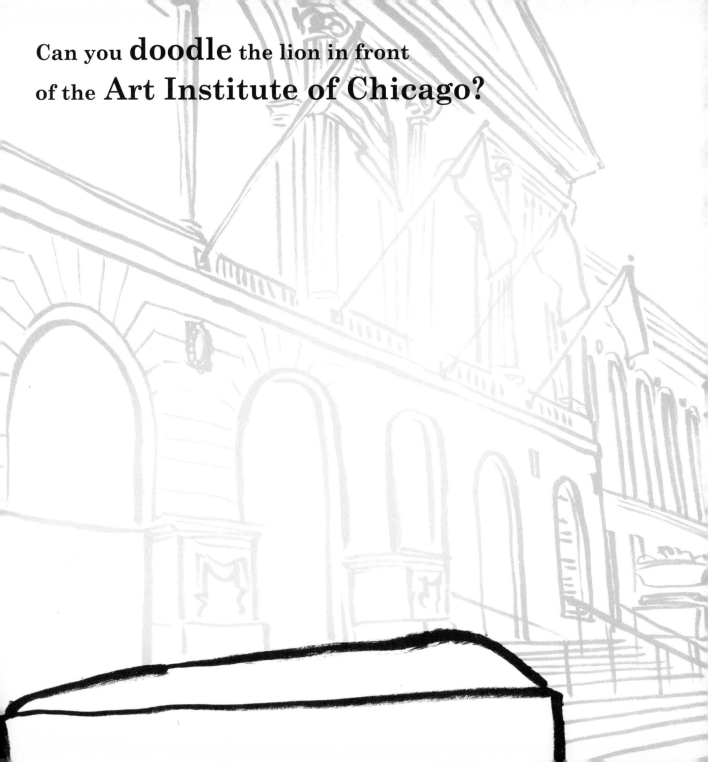

What will you dig up at the **Dinosaur Expedition?**
Doodle it!

You can uncover your own fossils at the Chicago Children's
Museum at Navy Pier.

What is your **favorite** football team?

Doodle the **name and number** of your favorite **Chicago Bulls** player.

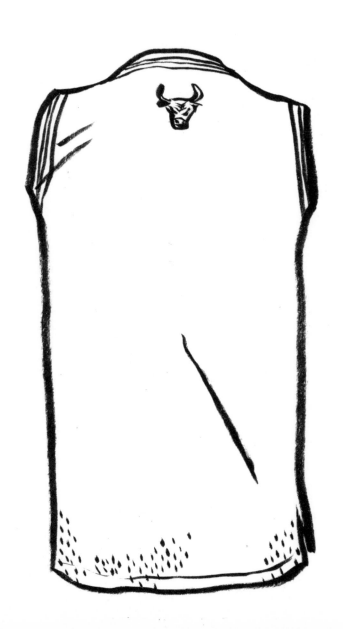

Take the **Doodle Challenge:**

The big bean is gone! What shape

would you make your sculpture to replace it? Doodle it!

Name of your creation _____

Color the **Chicago flag.**

Then, doodle your own design for a flag.

What color are the **autumn leaves?**
Add your own leaves to the **pile.**

The Chicago
city motto is *Urbs in
Horto,* which is Latin
for "City in a Garden."

It's a blizzard!

What are you going to do on this **snow day?**

Finish this **doodle** of the **Chicago Water Tower.**

The Water Tower was one of the only downtown buildings to survive the 1871 Chicago fire.

This **fireman** needs his **uniform.**

Scan this QR code
and get more Chicago
characters to color!

Who is coming through the **revolving door?**

Chicago has more revolving doors than
any other city in the United States.

Who's **guarding** the goal? **Doodle** a goalie—**fast!**

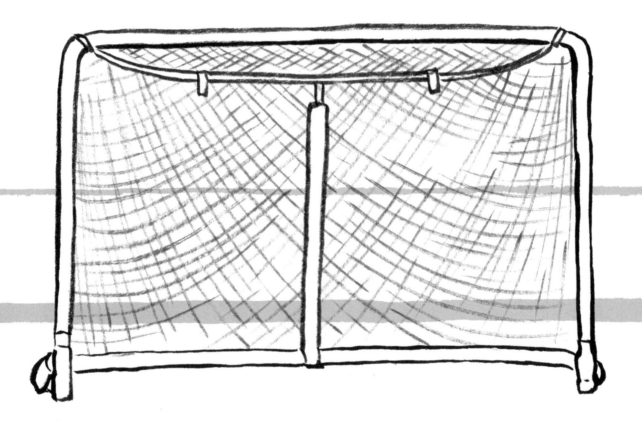

The Chicago Blackhawks play their home games
at the United Center.

What would you put on your **Day of the Dead** altar?

The National Museum of Mexican Art celebrates
the Day of the Dead every fall.

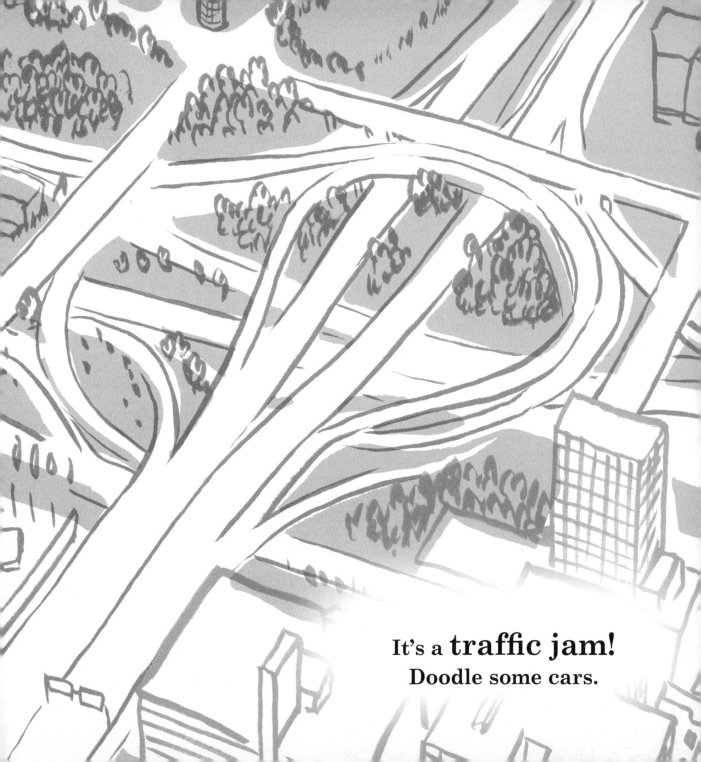

It's a **traffic jam!**
Doodle some cars.

Doodle some **constellations** in the sky.

The Adler Planetarium is a great place to explore the universe!

Decorate the **Christmas tree** in Daley Plaza.

Draw a car for the **Chicago Auto Show!**

The very first Chicago Auto Show was held in 1901.

These rooftops need bleachers. Doodle them.

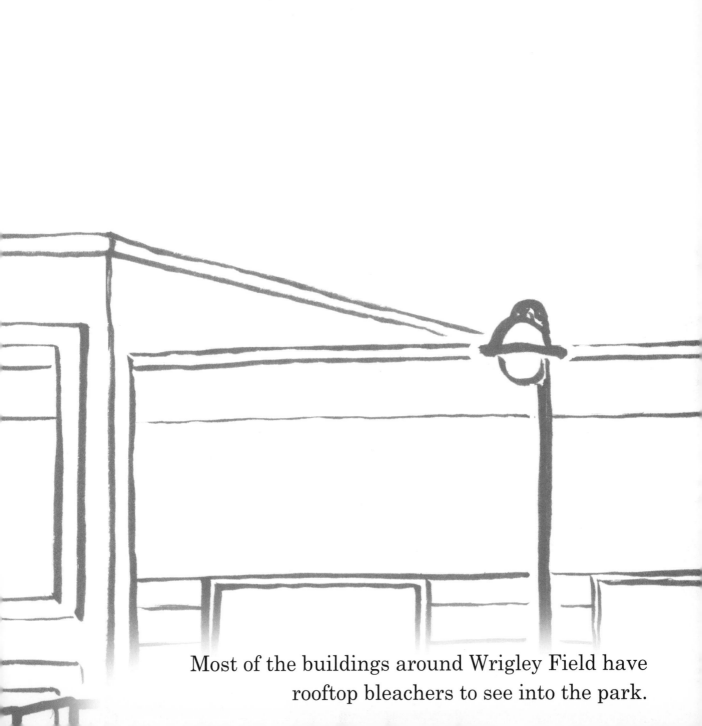

Most of the buildings around Wrigley Field have
rooftop bleachers to see into the park.

Draw **some cars** on both levels of the
Michigan Avenue Bridge.

The two-level Michigan Avenue Bridge can open
from the middle to let boats pass.

Doodle a water taxi.

You can catch a water taxi at many docks along the Chicago River.

What **books** did you find at the Printers Row Lit Fest?

Fill your photo album with **memories** of Chicago.

Can you finish the Willis Tower?